GEARED FOR GROWTH BIBLE STUDIES

UNDERSTANDING THE WAY OF

SALVATION

GOD'S PERFECT PLAN

BIBLE STUDIES TO IMPACT THE LIVES OF ORDINARY PEOPLE

The Word Worldwide

by Carol Jones

reaching the unreached

CHRISTIAN
FOCUS

ISBN 978-1-84550-713-8

Copyright © WEC International

Published in 2002, reprinted in 2011
by
Christian Focus Publications, Geanies House,
Fearn, Ross-shire, IV20 1TW, Scotland
www.christianfocus.com
and
WEC International, Bulstrode, Oxford Road,
Gerrards Cross, Bucks, SL9 8SZ
www.wecinternational.org

Cover design by Alister MacInnes

Printed and bound by Bell and Bain
Glasgow

Mixed Sources
Product group from well-managed
forests and other controlled sources
www.fsc.org Cert no. TT-COC-002769
© 1996 Forest Stewardship Council

Contents

PREFACE 4

INTRODUCTORY STUDY 5

STUDY 1 7

STUDY 2 10

STUDY 3 13

STUDY 4 16

STUDY 5 19

STUDY 6 22

STUDY 7 25

STUDY 8 29

STUDY 9 32

ANSWER GUIDE 36

GUIDE TO STUDY 1 37

GUIDE TO STUDY 2 38

GUIDE TO STUDY 3 39

GUIDE TO STUDY 4 40

GUIDE TO STUDY 5 41

GUIDE TO STUDY 6 42

GUIDE TO STUDY 7 43

GUIDE TO STUDY 8 44

GUIDE TO STUDY 9 45

PREFACE

**'Where there's LIFE there's GROWTH:
where there's GROWTH there's LIFE.'**

WHY GROW a study group?
Because as we study and share the Bible together, we can:
- learn to combat loneliness, depression, staleness, frustration and other problems,
- get to understand and love one another,
- become responsive to the Holy Spirit's dealing and obedient to God's Word,

and that's **GROWTH.**

HOW do you **GROW** a study group?
- Just start by asking one friend to join you and then aim at expanding your group.
- Study the set portions daily – they are brief and easy: no catches.
- Meet once a week to discuss what you find.
- Befriend others, and work away together.

see how it **GROWS.**

WHEN you GROW...
Things will happen at school, at home, at work, in your youth group, your student fellowship, women's meetings, midweek meetings, churches, communities, and so on.

You'll be **REACHING THROUGH TEACHING.**

WHEN you PRAY...
Remember those involved in writing and production of the study courses: pray for missionaries and nationals working on the translations into many different languages. Pray for groups studying that each member will not only be enriched personally, but will be reaching out continually to involve others. Pray for group leaders and those who direct the studies locally, nationally and internationally.

WHEN you PAY...
Realize that all profits from sales of studies go to develop the ministry on our mission fields and beyond, pay translators, and so on, and have the joy of knowing you are working together with them in the task.

INTRODUCTORY STUDY

Perhaps you have never read the Bible before, or if you have tried you may have found it difficult to understand. When the Bible was written it was written in the common language of the day, not in a language that people did not understand, but in the ordinary language of the people. Today we have many excellent translations of the Bible written in the language we speak every day, e.g., Good News Bible, Youth Bible, New International Version, etc. God wants us to understand His Word, Romans 10:17.

Note: When you see Romans 10:17, it means Romans chapter 10 verse 17. The Bible is divided into 66 Books, 39 in the Old Testament and 27 in the New Testament. The chart below will help you understand how the Old Testament Books and the New Testament Books are divided:

Old Testament

Genesis – Deuteronomy	Books of Moses (the laws are given here).
Joshua – Esther	History.
Job – Song of Songs	Poetry Books.
Isaiah – Daniel	Major Prophets.
Hosea – Malachi	Minor Prophets.

New Testament

Matthew – John	Gospels (from Jesus' birth to His ascension).
Acts	History of the Early Church.
Romans – Philemon	Paul's Letters (sent to churches and individuals).
Hebrews	Letter to Jewish Christians.
James – Jude	General Letters.
Revelation	Prophecy.

It helped me as a young Christian to learn these books of the Bible in song; perhaps it would help you too.

The Bible was written over a 1,600 year span, by over 40 authors. These were people from different times and backgrounds. Some were kings, prophets, shepherds, farmers, and fishermen. There was also a doctor and a tax collector. God used ordinary people from various walks of life, from different countries and backgrounds to write His Word. The Bible was written on three different continents: Asia, Africa and Europe; in three different languages: Hebrew, Greek and Aramaic; and on hundreds of different subjects. Most of these people never met and yet as we study more and more of the Word of God, it is amazingly accurate. Why is this? Acts 1:16; 2 Peter 1:21 and 2 Timothy 3:16 show us that the author is the Holy Spirit. No other book can be compared with the Bible. It is unique in every way because it is God speaking to us today.

The Bible has been read by more people and published in more languages than any other book. It has survived vicious attacks; some have banned it, burned it, outlawed it and tried to destroy it completely. If this book had not been the Book of God, men would have succeeded in destroying it many years ago, but the Bible is still loved and read today.

These studies are designed to help you begin to study the Bible for yourselves. At first you may have difficulty finding the verses. Don't worry about it or be embarrassed in your group. Remember no one is born with knowledge of the Bible. We all have to begin somewhere. Every Bible will have an index showing you where to find the various books. Use this as a reference until you are able to find your way around the Bible with ease.

I remember my first experience of being in a Bible Study when the leader said, 'Turn to Psalms'. I was so embarrassed because I didn't have a clue where the Book of Psalms was, or what it was. An older Christian whispered in my ear, 'Open your Bible in the middle and you'll find Psalms'. Everyone in the Bible Study was glad to help, and I learnt quite a lot in those Bible Studies because I was free to ask as many questions as I liked. As you meet week by week, be free to ask questions and give your opinion about the subject. In this way you will help each other.

Now turn to Psalm 119:103 and as you learn about and continue to read God's Word you will understand this verse more and more.

STUDY 1
SIN

QUESTIONS

DAY 1   Romans 5:12.
How did sin enter the world?

DAY 2   Genesis 3:1-6.
What did Adam and Eve do in these verses?

DAY 3   Romans 5:12, 19.
The sin that Adam committed, what effect has it had on us today?

DAY 4   Psalm 51:5.
When did sin enter our lives?

DAY 5   Matthew 15:19.
Where do these sins come from?

DAY 6   Psalm 139:23, 24.
        Are we willing to come honestly before God and ask Him to search
        our hearts and show us if there is anything that is wrong in our lives?

DAY 7   Proverbs 20:9.
        Is our self-effort the answer to a pure life before God?

NOTES

We began our study on sin by looking at its origin. Most of us know the story of Adam and Eve, and how Eve took that forbidden fruit and shared it with her husband. This is how sin entered into the world, through their disobedience to God. All mankind has inherited this sin. We all know how easy it is to sin and how hard it sometimes is not to sin. There are times when the temptation to sin can be too much for us and we easily fall.

We are living in a world that accepts as normal, sins that the Word of God condemns. In today's generation many of the sins named by Jesus in Matthew 15:19 are not considered to be sins at all. We hear people say, 'It's okay to live together if we're really in love', or, 'It's only a little white lie'. I remember my Pastor many years ago saying, 'It's a sin to steal a pin'.

Of course we see all around us the effect of sin in our world. Our prisons are bulging with so many offenders that the authorities are continually having to think of solutions to these problems. The drug problem (which causes many to steal, etc., to get their 'fix') continues despite all the advertising, medical help, rehabilitation centres and the like.

A few years ago I met a young woman who had been a heroin addict for eight years. This habit had changed her from being a well brought up public school girl to a criminal. When I first met her she had just been released from prison on bail. She was painfully thin; I was to find out later it was a miracle she was still alive. This young woman had desperately wanted to die because her heroin addiction had taken over her life. She drove herself onto some nearby moors, stopped the car and swallowed the contents of a bottle of paracetamol with a bottle of whisky. After a few hours she woke up and found that in her sleep she had vomited all the lethal contents from her stomach. Miraculously she had not died. She is now a joyful young woman who has been completely changed because the Lord has rescued her from her hopeless situation.

Are we willing to believe what God says about sin today and come before Him in honesty? We can't hide anything from Him anyway.

The conclusion of the matter is that we can do nothing about our sin. Try as we might, we will always fail. How many of us have broken New Year's resolutions quite early into the New Year, having failed in our efforts!

STUDY 2
GOD'S ANSWERS

QUESTIONS

DAY 1 John 3:16.
Why did God give His Son Jesus?

DAY 2 Romans 5:6-8.
Did Christ die for us when we had overcome sin in our lives or when we were helpless and still sinners?

DAY 3 Isaiah 53:5; 1 Peter 2:24.
a) Who are these verses talking about?

b) What are these verses describing?

DAY 4 Hebrews 9:22; Matthew 26:28.
Why did Jesus shed His blood?

DAY 5 Acts 3:19.
a) What does it mean to repent?

b) Will we be forgiven if we repent?

DAY 6   1 John 1:9.
        As we confess or admit our sins to God what will He do?

DAY 7   Acts 16:31; Acts 2:21.
        Looking back over today and the last few days, what are the steps
        we need to take in order to become Christians?

NOTES

We begin this week on a positive note, God's love. After last week's study we could easily have come to the conclusion that there is no hope for us – we are sinners and we can do nothing about it – BUT GOD CAN! Thank God that He saw our condition and had an answer for our problems, Jesus.

So many people think that they have to make themselves right before approaching God. Romans 5:6-8 tells us that Jesus died for us when we were helpless sinners. In Study 1 I told you the true story of a young woman who thought that the only way out of her sinful life was suicide. The truth was that the only way out for her was to call on the Lord Jesus Christ to save her. She called and He rescued her from that life of addiction and made her into the beautiful young woman she is today.

Some feel trapped and frustrated. They have an idea of what they ought to be and to do but find that they just cannot live up to their expectations. Try as they will, there is nothing they can do. What a relief, then, to hear that they are not expected to do anything except call out to God, just as they are and where they are, to save them. Christ has done everything and sets them free.

When Jesus died on the cross it may have looked to the people of that day as if He had failed. But He died for our sins on that cross; He was punished instead of us. On the cross Jesus made a wonderful exchange with us – He took our sins on Himself (all the sins of the world), and gave us His righteousness. A clean life in exchange for our sinful dirty lives. Quite a bargain!

What then in simple language is God asking us to do? He's saying, 'Own up, don't hide from Me anymore. I know the truth about you. Just come to Me and ask for the forgiveness that Jesus has bought for you on the cross and you will have a new, clean life in Me.'

God loves you. He's not out to expose you and condemn you but to give you a new beginning.

Have you called on the Lord Jesus to save you? If not, you might like to use the words of this prayer to do so. 'Lord Jesus Christ, I acknowledge that I am a sinner. I am truly sorry for my sins and I turn from them in repentance. I believe that you died on the cross for me. Come in to my life, Lord Jesus. I accept your free gift of eternal life. Cleanse me and take control of me. Help me live for You. Thank you, Lord Jesus.'

STUDY 3
CHANGED LIVES

QUESTIONS

DAY 1   John 3:6, 7.
In these verses becoming a Christian is described as being 'born again'. In your own words how can you best describe what has happened to you?

DAY 2   2 Corinthians 5:17.
a) What old things have gone from your life?

b) What does 'the new has come' mean to you?

DAY 3   Hebrews 10:16.
What has God written on our hearts and minds?

DAY 4   Deuteronomy 8:3; 1 Peter 2:2.
As babies cry for milk and men need bread, what is the spiritual food we need daily?

DAY 5   Revelation 3:20; James 4:8.
What is the Lord calling us to do in these verses?

DAY 6 Hebrews 10:25; Acts 2:42.
a) What do these verses tell us about fellowship with other believers?

b) What results from fellowship like this?

DAY 7 Matthew 10:32, 33.
a) Why is it so important to tell others about our love for the Lord?

b) What happens if we reject Him publicly?

NOTES

We all experience changes in our lives. Perhaps the birth of a baby! What a change this brings into our homes – everything now revolves around this new bundle of energy. Then there's the change from winter to spring, when instead of bleakness and darkness the spring brings light and colour. These natural changes are a delight, but the change that the Lord Jesus Christ makes in our lives is truly amazing.

This week we see the difference that Jesus makes in our lives. The young woman I mentioned previously has changed completely. Remember, all efforts to change her in the past had failed – God alone changes lives. Her longing for drugs left her. Instead she had a longing to read and to know God's Word. She spent time in prayer with the Lord alone and with others, and told everyone she met the great things that the Lord had done for her. What a changed life!

The words that Jesus used in John 3:6, 7 about being 'born again' are difficult for some people to understand. Jesus by the Holy Spirit gives us a new life when we accept Him into our lives as our Saviour. His new life in us changes us completely. Someone said that it was as if a light had been turned on in his life. He was now ashamed of some of the things he used to love in his old life.

There is a new awareness of sin and a new hunger for the things of God. This is the new life within and, where there is a new life, there is also a hunger. As soon as a baby is born it cries for food. This is a healthy hunger for his mother's milk. We too, as soon as we become Christians will experience a longing to know more of God's Word. The Bible will become alive to us, fellowship with God will be uppermost in our lives, and we will love to meet and have fellowship with God's people.

This will result in a longing to share our faith with our friends and families, and with others who have not been 'born again'. People will see a difference in our lives, and this new life within us will shine and be seen by others.

But there is more. Unseen by us, Jesus talks about us to His Father as we talk to our friends about Him.

STUDY 4
SATAN BRINGS DOUBTS

QUESTIONS

DAY 1   John 1:12.
         As soon as we receive Jesus whose children are we?

DAY 2   Romans 8:15.
         a) What does the devil try to do in our lives?

         b) We are now God's children, so how close is our relationship to God?

DAY 3   Ephesians 2:19.
         What is your new position in God?

DAY 4   Galatians 4:7; John 10:10.
         In these two verses list what the devil would do in our lives and what
            God has done.

DAY 5   Revelation 12:10.
         a) Who is the accuser of our brothers?

b) Have you experienced accusations from the devil? Perhaps he has put doubts in your mind, for example, that the Lord has not accepted you.

c) Are these accusations common?

DAY 6   Revelation 12:11.
          How do you overcome the devil's accusations and doubts?

DAY 7   John 16:33.
          a) Who has overcome the world?

          b) What encouragement does this verse give us?

NOTES

We need to know who we are in Christ soon after we become Christians. Satan commonly attacks God's children with doubts – telling us such things as, 'You're not a Christian', 'God has not accepted you', or, 'You're not good enough'. This is not surprising as the name 'Satan' means 'Opponent' or 'Adversary'. He does all he can to hinder God's children.

We need to recognise that these lies are from Satan and learn to counteract them with the Word of God. Stand on what God's Word says. Learn some of the verses you have already studied so that you can come against any doubt with the Word of God.

The truth is, Satan is not happy that you have become a Christian, so all these doubts and fears are common to all Christians. You may think that you are the only one experiencing these fears and may keep quiet about it. If you are going through hard experiences like these, don't be afraid to share your feelings with an older Christian. They understand and will be glad to help you. Satan loves to keep you quiet by telling you that you are alone on this one and no one else will understand. Don't believe him. Tell someone and get it sorted out.

Remember that you are now God's child, an heir. Imagine being an heir of God! He is your Father so don't be overwhelmed when you are attacked like this. You are not the only one to experience this. God's Word stands forever, use it as your foundation.

Our first feeling after becoming a Christian is usually one of joy. Sometimes people even feel as if they're walking on air (don't worry if you have not had this experience). After a while if these feelings subside we may begin to wonder if God has left us. We have to learn to follow the Lord not by our feelings but by faith in His Word, because our feelings change but God is always the same. Of course our feelings of joy will return, but at low times in our lives Satan can lie to us and tell us that God has left us. A little rhyme I learnt when I was a young Christian has helped me many times:

> 'Be my feelings what they will,
> Jesus is my Saviour still.'

STUDY 5
OBEDIENCE TO GOD'S WORD

QUESTIONS

DAY 1   Joshua 1:8.
        a) What are we told to do with God's Word?

        b) What will be the result of this obedience?

DAY 2   Matthew 7:24, 25.
        a) What should be our response to God's Word?

        b) When the problems of life (represented by the rain and wind) beat against us, how can we cope?

DAY 3   Matthew 22:36-38.
        a) How much are we to love God?

        b) Ask yourself the question, do I really love God like this?

DAY 4   John 15:17.
        How easy do we find it to obey this command?

DAY 5 1 John 5:2, 3.
a) If we love God how will this show in our lives?

b) What can we discover about God's commands for us?

DAY 6 Colossians 3:13; Luke 23:33, 34.
a) How strong is God's requirement that we are to forgive others?

b) What did Jesus cry from the cross?

c) If Jesus could forgive such injustice and cruelty, can we not forgive?

DAY 7 1 Corinthians 11:23-26; Acts 2:38.
What two commands are believers asked to obey in the above verses?

NOTES

Before we are able to obey the Lord we must read His Word in order to know what He requires of us. Our study this week shows the most important commands that the Lord gives us. Of course, as we read more of His Word we will discover for ourselves other steps of obedience we may need to take.

Remember that God's commands are for our good. He wants the best for us in our lives, so obedience to Him will give a life of fulfilment and satisfaction. If we love God as He asks us to, then we will want to please Him in every detail. If we have wronged somebody or have not forgiven someone, this will trouble us until we put things right with him or her.

Two important things that the Lord asks us to keep are the communion service (breaking of bread) and baptism. We should be careful to obey God in these and then we will know His blessing. Do note, however, that different branches of the Christian church observe baptism and communion in different ways. Be careful not to be drawn into fruitless discussions with those whose practices may be different from yours.

To go on with God means a life of obedience to Him. Unfortunately, many have come to a dead end in their Christian lives because of disobedience to God's Word, e.g., refusing to forgive someone who has wronged them. I know that this can be very difficult at times, but the Lord will help us if we ask Him.

God's Word can be very challenging and can sometimes make us feel very uncomfortable. I remember as a young Christian continually reading the verse in Matthew 5:14-16, which tells us not to hide our faith, but to show everyone that we love Jesus. This verse really upset me because as a youngster I did not want to share my faith with my friends in case they laughed at me. I struggled with this verse for quite a while until I was able to obey God and tell others about Him. The result was that even though some of my friends left me, others became Christians. What a delight it was as a young Christian to lead others to the Lord!

As you are reading this you may be saying, 'You don't know what has happened to me – how can I ever forgive? I have been hurt too much.' God knows how much you have been hurt. Ask Him to start helping you to forgive. Begin by saying that although you feel no forgiveness at all, you are willing to be made willing to forgive. This will begin to free you from being bitter and will help heal that hurt in your heart.

STUDY 6
PRAYER

QUESTIONS

DAY 1   Matthew 6:9; Philippians 4:6b.
a) To whom do we pray?

b) What relationship do we have with God?

DAY 2   Philippians 4:6; 1 Peter 5:7.
a) What do we bring to God in prayer?

b) What do we know from 1 Peter 5:7?

DAY 3   Matthew 6:5-8.
a) Where does verse 6 tell us to pray?

b) What does Jesus tell us in verse 7?

c) What does verse 8 tell us about God?

DAY 4   Luke 18:1-8.
a) What did the woman in the parable do?

b) Why did the unjust judge answer her?

c) Think how different God is, will He answer us?

DAY 5 Jeremiah 32:27; Luke 1:37; Ephesians 3:20.
   a) What do we learn about God in the first two of these verses?

   b) Think about what we ask of God in the light of Ephesians 3:20.

DAY 6 Luke 11:9; Isaiah 65:24.
   a) List the results of asking, seeking and knocking.

   b) How can God answer before we finish praying? (Remember Matthew 6:8.)

DAY 7 James 4:3; Matthew 7:9-11.
   a) Do we always get what we pray for?

   b) Why not?

   c) What can we say about the things which God does give us?

NOTES

One day one of the disciples asked Jesus, 'Lord teach us to pray' (Luke 11:1). Through the gospels Jesus teaches us to pray by His example and also by His teaching on prayer. We can pour out our hearts to God telling Him things we could not share with anyone else. And why not! He knows all about us anyway. Even the hairs on our head are numbered (Luke 12:7). Not only does He know everything, He also cares about us and is able to answer our prayers.

The study this week encourages us to talk to the Lord about everything in our lives and to pray for others. God answers prayer but not always in the way we expect. We must also wait for God to answer us. We see that just as any father would refuse to give his child anything harmful, so our Heavenly Father is the same. We can trust Him because He always wants the best for us.

Sometimes our prayers to God are 'emergency prayers'. I am reminded of a time when we were travelling to Romania in two vehicles. One was a converted bus full of aid and the other a large van carrying valuable medical supplies. The van began making an awful noise, so we limped into the next town where we thought we could get help. We were a 'mixed bunch' on board. Some were Christians and some were not. One of the non-Christians challenged us to pray and ask 'our' God to help us – so we did. As soon as we had finished praying a young man came up to us and asked if we needed help. He was a Christian from the local Baptist Church. He helped us take the van into the church enclosure where it would be safe, and then arranged for a mechanic to repair it. This was a wonderful answer to prayer, because as soon as the van entered the enclosure it came to a complete stop! If this van had stopped anywhere else and been left, it would most certainly have been looted. The van was repaired and its contents given to a hospital.

You will find that time spent in prayer is never wasted, and the more time you spend in secret before your Father the more time you will want to spend in His presence. Prayer is our lifeline; we cannot survive in this world without it. The more time you spend with a person, the more like him or her you become – the Bible teaches us also that if we spend time with an angry person then we too will pick up his angry ways. So let us spend time before the Lord in prayer and we too will become more like Him.

STUDY 7

GUIDANCE

QUESTIONS

DAY 1   Matthew 6:10; Matthew 26:42.
a) Why did Jesus teach us to pray, 'your will be done ...'?

b) Was it easy for Jesus to say, 'may your will be done'?

c) The best way is sometimes a costly way. Are we willing to accept God's way for our lives?

DAY 2   Psalm 25:9.
a) Who does the Lord lead in this verse?

b) How would you describe the humble person here?

DAY 3   John 16:13.
a) Who is Jesus referring to in this verse?

b) What is the Holy Spirit's work as seen in this verse?

DAY 4 Psalm 119:105; Psalm 119:9.

      a) Where does our guidance come from?

      b) Why is the Word compared to a lamp?

DAY 5 Psalm 5:8; Matthew 2:13.

      a) Why do we need the Lord's guidance?

      b) How did God warn and guide Joseph?

      c) What was the purpose of God's guidance here?

DAY 6 Isaiah 42:16.

      a) Where does the Lord promise to lead us?

      b) As He guides us, what will be different?

      c) List all the 'I will' statements in this verse and think about their meaning.

DAY 7 Acts 16:6-10; Romans 8:14.

      a) In Acts 16:6-8 what was happening to Paul and his companions?

b) Has this ever happened to you?

c) What is the difference in Acts 16:9-10?

d) What can we learn from these verses?

NOTES

The Lord can never guide us unless we are willing to yield to Him completely. If we want to go our own way or do our own thing in life we will not even consider asking the Lord for guidance. We all at some time or another have important decisions to make, and we need the Lord's guidance in order to make the right choices. As we yield our lives to Him we will want His will in everything we do. As we grow as Christians to know Him more, we will grow to trust Him because His ways are always the best.

Guidance, therefore, starts with us seeking God's will for our lives. As we can see from these studies, He guides us to protect us from harm. He will always lead us in the way of truth; He will never mislead us. As we ask Him, He will show us. We can depend on Him. These verses from Scripture show that the Lord uses various ways to lead His people. He is the same God today and will show us clearly which way He wants us to go. Always use the Word of God (Bible) as your 'plumb line'. The Lord will never guide us contrary to His Word.

It can be very exciting at times to know God's guidance in our lives; He guides us in the big things of life as well as in the small details. Recently I went on holiday with a few of my friends and we decided to take with us Gospels of Matthew and John, and New Testaments in the language of the people of that country. We prayed together and asked the Lord for guidance. We wanted to give God's Word to the right people. I also asked the Lord to guide us to a Christian (which seemed an impossibility being away from the large towns). We were visiting quite a remote area in the south-west of the country when I saw some ladies selling lace. The Lord led me to give one of them a Gospel of Matthew; I had been very reluctant to do so because of the possibility of being arrested. The elderly lady took the gospel and held it high, waving it above her head, showing everyone around her what she had received. This made me fearful and I wanted to run, but another lady came and begged me for a copy, so I gave her a Gospel of John. She ran into her home and brought out a Christian picture tract. She pointed to her heart and then to heaven, and made me understand that she was a Christian. Her delight to receive a part of God's Word in her own language was clear. Thank you, Lord, for your guidance.

Remember the promises in Isaiah 42:16. Stand on these promises and wait for God to open the right door for you.

STUDY 8
IN HIS SERVICE

QUESTIONS

DAY 1   John 1:41, 45.
   a) What were Andrew and Philip doing?

   b) Are you telling your family and friends, etc., about Jesus?

   c) Do you find it difficult to share about Jesus?

DAY 2   Acts 1:8; Luke 24:49.
   a) What was the promise of the Father?

   b) How would the Holy Spirit's power affect them?

DAY 3   Acts 2:1-4; Acts 2:14-17; Acts 2:41.
   a) Did God keep His promise here?

   b) What was the result?

   c) What was the result of Peter's preaching?

   d) Do we need the Holy Spirit's power to witness today?

DAY 4   Acts 18:9-10.
        a) What can fear do to us?

        b) What, in this verse, encourages us to witness?

DAY 5   Ezekiel 3:18-19.
        a) What serious warning do we get in these verses?

        b) If we tell them and they do not listen to us, what then?

DAY 6   2 Kings 7:9 (chapters 6 and 7 can be read to get the whole story);
        Acts 4:20.
        a) Would the lepers have been wrong to keep back the good news?

        b) How do these verses speak into our situation?

DAY 7   John 9:4; Ecclesiastes 9:10; Romans 12:1.
        a) List what we are encouraged to do in these verses.

        b) Why?

        c) What do you think God meant by 'living sacrifices'?

NOTES

The Bible tells us that those who win souls are wise. We are saved to serve. As soon as we became Christians the Lord could have taken us immediately to heaven. Why didn't He? Why does He leave us on earth? We are here mainly to witness to others. How will they know about the Lord if we don't tell them?

When Jesus was on earth He promised to send the Holy Spirit to be with us always. The power of the Holy Spirit gives us strength and wisdom to witness to others. The Holy Spirit gives us the words to speak, takes these words, and uses them to convict those to whom we are speaking. We need to ask Jesus to fill us with the Holy Spirit and make us shine for God in this dark world.

As we see needs around us, perhaps those of our family and close friends, we will have compassion and concern for them. As Christians we can introduce them to the One (Jesus) who loves them and died for them. We cannot keep what He has done for us a secret.

Sometimes it is hard to witness. We may be laughed at, etc., but we need to lay down our lives as 'living sacrifices' and work for God while we are able, because one day it will be too late. I remember listening to a missionary telling about a dream he had. He dreamt that he was in heaven watching crowds of people standing before God on the day of judgment. From the crowd a condemned man pointed a bony finger at him and said, 'I never heard about Jesus. You didn't tell me!' When this man woke up he was so convicted that he spent the rest of his life as a missionary in India.

We always need to have wisdom (Jas. 1:5 and 3:17) when telling others about Jesus. Don't corner people or argue. We can win arguments but lose souls. Everyone you speak to will be different, so ask the Holy Spirit to guide you into saying the right things.

Remember too that your life can speak louder that your words. Live a life that brings glory to the Lord. The people you live with or work with know you; they see your actions and your reactions. Ask the Lord to give you His special love for those around you, so that they see not only from your words but also from your life that Jesus is alive in you. Remember, you preach the gospel every day by how you live and treat others.

STUDY 9
DAILY LIVING

QUESTIONS

DAY 1   John 15:4-5; 2 John 9.
   a) In John 15:4 what are we encouraged to do?

   b) What is the natural outcome of this?

   c) 2 John 9 gives us a strong warning. Why?

DAY 2   Genesis 6:9; Galatians 5:22-23.
   a) Why was Noah a righteous and blameless man?

   b) How do you think the fruit of the Spirit is produced?

DAY 3   Psalm 145:18; Acts 17:27.
   a) How do we speak or call to the Lord?

   b) Why does Acts 17:27 encourage us?

   c) Do you find it easy to speak to God?

DAY 4 Psalm 1:1-2; Isaiah 40:8.
  a) From where does this man get his advice?

  b) From whom do we seek advice?

  c) How often does this man read God's Word?

  d) How permanent is God's Word?

DAY 5 Romans 12:2; Ephesians 4:22, 24; Romans 6:11.
  a) What does God want to change in us?

  b) How does this new life show itself?

  c) What does Romans 6:11 mean to you in your daily life?

DAY 6 Proverbs 3:5-6.
  a) What do these verses encourage us to do?

  b) What often happens to us when we rely on ourselves?

  c) What happens when we turn to God in everything?

DAY 7 Matthew 28:20; Romans 8:38-39; Hebrews 13:5; Deuteronomy 31:6.
        a) What positive promises do we have in these verses?

        b) How do these promises make us feel?

        c) Who is able to make such promises to us?

NOTES

Now that we are Christians we need to walk daily with the Lord. What does this mean? This week we discover the answer and learn how to keep close to the Lord every day.

Jesus calls us to stay close to Him. He compared Himself to a vine and us to the branches of that vine. The branch produces fruit because it is attached to the vine. If it is broken away it cannot produce any fruit on its own. We too cannot live the Christian life by our own self-effort. We will only grow and produce the fruit (Gal. 5:22, 23) as we walk with the Lord every day.

If you want to keep up a friendship you have to remain in contact with your friend, speaking and listening to him or her. In the same way we have to speak to the Lord in prayer and read His Word on a daily basis. Soon we will know that He is our Friend as well as our Saviour, and we will love to spend that quiet time in His presence.

We will see the result of our friendship with Him even in the way we think and the way we act. Our minds will begin to see things as He sees them and not as we used to see and react. So then we will seek His approval in everything we do. It is so good to know the God who loves us, who has the best for us in our lives.

There will of course be times when we will make mistakes and perhaps feel too ashamed to come to the Lord. Don't stay away from God in times like these. He is ready to listen and forgive.

Our reading on DAY 7 reminds us that the Lord is always with us. We may have been hurt and disappointed when friends have left us, or perhaps we have lost someone close to us through death. Remember the Lord has promised that He will never leave us and is able always to keep His promises.

You have begun your walk with God! Life will be very different for you from now on. As you continue to share your faith with others they will begin to ask questions about the Bible. Our next set of studies will be about knowing who God is, who Jesus is, and who the Holy Spirit is. These studies will help you get to know more about God for yourself and also to be able to answer those awkward questions that others ask you. May God bless you as you seek Him more and more in His Word.

ANSWER GUIDE

The following pages contain an Answer Guide. It is recommended that answers to the questions be attempted before turning to this guide. It is only a guide and the answers given should not be treated as exhaustive.

GUIDE TO STUDY 1

DAY 1

Through one man (Adam).

DAY 2

Listened to the serpent (Satan) and disobeyed God by eating the
forbidden fruit.

DAY 3

We all became sinners.

DAY 4

When our mother conceived us.

DAY 5

From the heart or within us.

DAY 6

Personal.

DAY 7

No, we always fail.

GUIDE TO STUDY 2

DAY 1

Because He loved the world.

DAY 2

When we were helpless and still sinners.

DAY 3

a) Jesus Christ.
b) Jesus being crucified (being punished for our sins).

DAY 4

So that our sins might be forgiven.

DAY 5

a) Turning from our sins and turning to God.
b) Yes, we will be completely forgiven.

DAY 6

Forgive us and make us clean.

DAY 7

We need to confess our sins, repent of them, believe that Jesus was punished for our sins and call on the Lord (pray).

GUIDE TO STUDY 3

DAY 1

Individual answer – there is a difference between the natural life which we all live and the new spiritual life we have in God since we became Christians.

DAY 2

a) Personal – think about this and give examples from your own life.
b) The life of the Lord Jesus.

DAY 3

His law. A new awareness of what is good and what is evil.

DAY 4

We need daily to read and take in God's Word.

DAY 5

The Lord seeks fellowship with us, He calls us in these verses to open the door and to come near to Him (a daily walk).

DAY 6

a) Not to give up meeting together but to be loyal to the fellowship.
b) We are encouraged in our faith as we learn from God's Word, pray and have fellowship together.

DAY 7

a) Jesus will then do the same before the Father in heaven.
b) He will reject us before His Father. Our denial of Jesus means that we were never really His. It does not mean we can lose our salvation.

GUIDE TO STUDY 4

DAY 1

God's children.

DAY 2

a) Make us a slave and cause us to be afraid (bring doubts into our lives).
b) So close that we can call Him Abba Father, which is what a child would call his father (daddy).

DAY 3

A member of God's family and fellow citizen with God's people.

DAY 4

The devil makes us slaves. He is a thief coming to steal, kill and destroy. God makes us sons and heirs. He has come to give us life to the full.

DAY 5

a) The devil.
b) Personal.
c) Yes, very common. The devil accuses day and night.

DAY 6

Claiming the protection from the blood of the Lamb; by believing God's Word to us and speaking it out.

DAY 7

a) Jesus.
b) To be brave – despite troubles we will have peace by being united to Him.

GUIDE TO STUDY 5

DAY 1

    a) Study it and obey it.
    b) God's blessing.

DAY 2

    a) We must believe and obey His Word.
    b) By believing God's promises we will stand and not fall in times of trouble.

DAY 3

    a) With all (not a part) of our heart, soul and mind.
    b) Personal.

DAY 4

    Personal.

DAY 5

    a) We will carry out His commands and love the children of God.
    b) They are not too hard.

DAY 6

    a) It is a commandment.
    b) Father forgive them.
    c) Personal.

DAY 7

    Observe the Lord's Supper (Communion, Breaking of Bread) and Baptism.

GUIDE TO STUDY 6

DAY 1
>   a) God.
>   b) He is our heavenly Father.

DAY 2
>   a) Everything – all we need.
>   b) He cares for us so we can give Him all our worries.

DAY 3
>   a) In the privacy of our own rooms.
>   b) To talk to God simply.
>   c) That He knows everything we need before we even ask Him.

DAY 4
>   a) She kept asking, she was persistent.
>   b) Because she kept bothering him.
>   c) Own answer – do you believe He will answer your prayers?

DAY 5
>   a) There is nothing too difficult for God.
>   b) Personal.

DAY 6
>   a) You will receive, find, and the door will be opened.
>   b) He knows our need before we ask Him.

DAY 7
>   a) No.
>   b) We sometimes ask with wrong motives, things we want that are not good for us.
>   c) He won't give us anything that will harm us – only the best.

GUIDE TO STUDY 7

DAY 1

a) Because God's will is always the best way for us.
b) No – it was very costly.
c) Personal.

DAY 2

a) The humble.
b) One who is willing to be taught God's will.

DAY 3

a) The Holy Spirit.
b) To lead us into all that is true and tell us of things to come.

DAY 4

a) God's Word (Bible).
b) Because it is a light for our path in our daily walk.

DAY 5

a) Because of our enemies' plans against us.
b) An angel appeared to him in a dream.
c) To protect the infant Christ from harm.

DAY 6

a) On roads we have not yet travelled.
b) From darkness to light, rough places made smooth.
c) Actual wording will depend on the translation used: I will lead, I will guide; I will turn darkness to light; I will make rough places (country) smooth; I will keep my promises; I will not forsake them.

DAY 7

a) The Holy Spirit was guiding them by closing doors.
b) Personal.
c) Here God called Paul to preach in Macedonia (open door).
d) As God's sons He will lead us sometimes by closing doors, at other times by clear visions and open doors.

GUIDE TO STUDY 8

DAY 1
>   a) Telling others (family members) about Jesus.
>   b) Personal.
>   c) Personal.

DAY 2
>   a) The power of the Holy Spirit.
>   b) They would be witnesses at home and abroad.

DAY 3
>   a) Yes – the Holy Spirit came.
>   b) Peter witnessed in power (before this he was afraid).
>   c) Three thousand were saved.
>   d) Yes we do!

DAY 4
>   a) Stop us speaking, keep us silent.
>   b) The Lord is with us, we need not be afraid to speak.

DAY 5
>   a) We will be held responsible if we have not warned those who live in sin.
>   b) We will not be held responsible for their reaction to the message.

DAY 6
>   a) Completely wrong and very selfish.
>   b) Personal.

DAY 7
>   a) Work while it is day, work hard at whatever you do, offer ourselves as living sacrifices to God.
>   b) Because when the night, or death comes, it will be too late to work for God.
>   c) Discuss this.

GUIDE TO STUDY 9

DAY 1

    a) To remain or stay with Jesus.
    b) Fruitfulness.
    c) We need to know that we can't go it alone – we need to stay close to Jesus.

DAY 2

    a) Because he lived in fellowship with God.
    b) By living close to God (Jesus).

DAY 3

    a) In sincerity, tell Him honestly how we feel.
    b) It tells us that when we look for Him we find Him because He is not far from us.
    c) Personal.

DAY 4

    a) Not from evil men, but from God's Word.
    b) Personal.
    c) Day and night.
    d) It stands for ever.

DAY 5

    a) Our minds.
    b) In a holy and true life.
    c) Personal (think of yourself as dead to sin, but living in God).

DAY 6

    a) To trust the Lord with all your heart and remember Him in everything we do.
    b) We often fail.
    c) He leads us in the right way.

DAY 7

    a) He will be with us always. Nothing can separate us from His love. He will never leave us or abandon us. The Lord God Himself will be with us, He will not fail us.
    b) Personal (secure and safe).
    c) Others can't, only God can.

GEARED FOR GROWTH BIBLE STUDIES

You can obtain a full list of over 50 'Geared for Growth' studies and order online at:

Our UK Website:
                        www.gearedforgrowth.co.uk

or why not look us up on Facebook

International enquiries should contact:
                        word.worldwideinternational@gmail.com

Further information can also be obtained from:

                        info@gearedforgrowth.co.uk

                        orders@gearedforgrowth.co.uk

                        www.christianfocus.com

Find out more about WEC INTERNATIONAL at www.wec.int.org.uk or on Facebook

Christian Focus Publications

Publishes books for all ages

Our mission statement –

STAYING FAITHFUL

In dependence upon God we seek to help make His infallible Word, the Bible, relevant. Our aim is to ensure the Lord Jesus Christ is presented as the only hope to obtain forgiveness of sin and live a useful life and look forward to heaven with Him.

REACHING OUT

Christian Focus Publications reaches out to each old and new age with the gospel message through their publishing books that point people towards Jesus and help them to develop a Christ-like maturity. We aim to reach all levels of reader for life, work, ministry and leisure.

Books in our four range are published in three imprints:

Christian Focus contains popular works including biographies, commentaries, basic doctrine and Christian living. Our children's books are published in this imprint.

Mentor focuses on books written at a level suitable for Bible College and seminary students, pastors, and other serious readers. The imprint includes commentaries, doctrinal studies, examination of current issues and church history.

Heritage contains classic writings from the past.

For details of our titles visit us on our website:
www.christianfocus.com